BASKETBALL SUPER STATS

JEFF SAVAGE

Lerner Publications ◆ Minneapolis

Statistics are through the 2015–2016 NBA and WNBA seasons.

Lerner Publications Company
A division of Lerner Publishing Group, Inc.
241 First Avenue North
Minneapolis, MN 55401 USA

For reading levels and more information, look up this title at www.lernerbooks.com.

Main body text set in Aptifer Sans LT Pro 12/18.
Typeface provided by Linotype AG.

Library of Congress Cataloging-in-Publication Data

Names: Savage, Jeff, 1961– author.
Title: Basketball Super Stats / Jeff Savage.
Description: Minneapolis, Minnesota : Lerner Publications, 2017. | Series: Pro Sports
    Stats | Includes bibliographical references and index. | Audience: Age 8–12. |
    Audience: Grade 4 to 6.
Identifiers: LCCN 2016045748 (print) | LCCN 2016054909 (ebook) | ISBN
    9781512434101 (lb : alk. paper) | ISBN 9781512449457 (eb pdf)
Subjects: LCSH: Basketball—Records—Juvenile literature. | Basketball—History—
    Juvenile literature.
Classification: LCC GV885.45 .S38 2017 (print) | LCC GV885.45 (ebook) | DDC
    796.323—dc23

LC record available at https://lccn.loc.gov/2016045748

Manufactured in the United States of America
1-42046-23916-1/17/2017

TABLE OF CONTENTS

PEACH BASKETS

On December 21, 1891, a physical education teacher in Springfield, Massachusetts, named James Naismith showed his class a game he had just invented. Naismith nailed a peach basket to the balcony at each end of the gym and divided his class into two teams of nine players each. The object of the game was to throw a ball into one of the fruit baskets. The players used a soccer ball, and the game lasted 30 minutes. William R. Chase scored the game's first—and only—basket. Chase's basket was the first statistic ever recorded in a basketball game.

JAMES NAISMITH

Fans use statistics, or stats, to measure and compare the performances of players and teams. Stats can show everything from how good a player is at shooting **free throws** to what kinds of shots are most likely to help a team beat an opponent. What are basketball's most important statistics? First, you should know how the rules of the game have changed over time. These changes have affected how stats are recorded and how fans respond to the game.

A SLOWER GAME

Early basketball games often had low scores. The games moved more slowly than modern National Basketball Association (NBA) games. The peach baskets had bottoms, so each time a shot went in, someone had to climb a ladder to get the ball. Baskets with an open bottom were not used until 1912. Before 1954 NBA games didn't use a **shot clock**. Teams would often stop shooting once they took the lead so that the other team would have fewer chances to score. But in 1954, the league began to use a 24-second shot clock. This forced teams to shoot more often and score more points. A year later, the Boston Celtics became the first team to average 100 points per game for a season. Four years after that, every team in the league averaged more than 100.

1955 BOSTON CELTICS

CHAPTER ONE

PLAYER SUPER STATS

A. C. GREEN

JUST A MINUTE, PLEASE

A. C. Green played in 1,192 straight games in his career. During this streak, he played for the Los Angeles Lakers, Phoenix Suns, Dallas Mavericks, and Miami Heat. Green holds the NBA record for most games played in a row. No wonder his Twitter handle is @NBA_Ironman!

An NBA season consists of 82 games for each team. But most NBA players don't play every game as Green did for so long. Some only play for a few minutes per game. If you want to know how much someone really played in a career, check out the minutes played stat. It shows how many minutes players spent on the court rather than how many games they played.

Most Minutes Played in a Career

PLAYER	TEAM*	MINUTES PLAYED
Kareem Abdul-Jabbar	Los Angeles Lakers	57,446
Karl Malone	Utah Jazz	54,852
Kevin Garnett	Minnesota Timberwolves	50,418
Jason Kidd	Dallas Mavericks	50,111
Elvin Hayes	Washington Bullets	50,000

*The player spent most of his career with this team.

TRIPLE DIGITS

On March 2, 1962, Wilt Chamberlain of the Philadelphia Warriors scored 100 points in a game. No one else has come close to matching that total. Chamberlain made 36 baskets and 28 free throws against the New York Knicks in a 169–147 Philadelphia win.

A player has scored 60 points or more in a game only 65 times in NBA history. Kobe Bryant (six times), Michael Jordan (five times), and Elgin Baylor (four times) were scoring machines. So what does that make Chamberlain? He did it 32 times!

HISTORY HIGHLIGHT

Kareem Abdul-Jabbar is the NBA's all-time leader in points scored and has won more Most Valuable Player (MVP) awards than anyone else. He was great in college too. In 1966, in his first varsity game for the University of California, Los Angeles (UCLA), he scored 56 points. He was so dominant near the basket that the National Collegiate Athletic Association (NCAA) outlawed slam dunks for a decade.

Most Points Scored in a Game

Wilt Chamberlain • Philadelphia Warriors • March 2, 1962

Kobe Bryant • Los Angeles Lakers • January 22, 2006

Wilt Chamberlain • Philadelphia Warriors • December 8, 1961

David Thompson • Denver Nuggets • April 9, 1978

Wilt Chamberlain • San Francisco Warriors • November 16, 1962

Wilt Chamberlain • Philadelphia Warriors • January 13, 1962

Wilt Chamberlain • San Francisco Warriors • November 3, 1962

David Robinson • San Antonio Spurs • April 24, 1994

Elgin Baylor • Los Angeles Lakers • November 15, 1960

Wilt Chamberlain • San Francisco Warriors • March 10, 1963

Player • Team • Date

70 72 74 76 78 80 82 84 86 88 90 92 94 96 98 100

Number of points

WILT THE STILT

Wilt Chamberlain was a superstar 7-foot 1-inch (2.2-meter) center at the University of Kansas who wanted to earn money playing basketball. But the NBA did not accept college players until their class had graduated. So Chamberlain left college a year early to play for the Harlem Globetrotters, an independent team known for performing tricks and comedic routines on the court. The following year, Chamberlain joined the NBA and scored 43 points in his first game. Most **rookies** score only a few points in their first games—if they play at all.

STATS FACT

Wilt Chamberlain scored 37.6 points per game his first season in the NBA and is still the only Rookie of the Year ever to lead the league in scoring average.

Highest Scoring Average per Game in a Season

Player • Team • Season

- Wilt Chamberlain • Philadelphia Warriors • 1961–1962
- Wilt Chamberlain • San Francisco Warriors • 1962–1963
- Wilt Chamberlain • Philadelphia Warriors • 1960–1961
- Wilt Chamberlain • Philadelphia Warriors • 1959–1960
- Michael Jordan • Chicago Bulls • 1986–1987

34 36 38 40 42 44 46 48 50 52

Points per game

HISTORY HIGHLIGHT

Many fans consider Michael Jordan the greatest basketball player of all time. He has won more awards than any other player in the NBA. He won the MVP award three times and led the Chicago Bulls to three NBA championships before retiring after the 1992–1993 season. Then he came back to the Bulls in 1994–1995 to win two more MVP awards and three more championships.

SCORING SPECIALISTS

Scoring is one of the most important stats to fans and teams. What does it take to be a high scorer at basketball's highest level? It takes a shot that cannot be blocked, like Kareem Abdul-Jabbar's skyhook. Or it takes Michael Jordan's will to win or Shaquille O'Neal's dominant physical presence. The greatest scorers in the NBA all had something special.

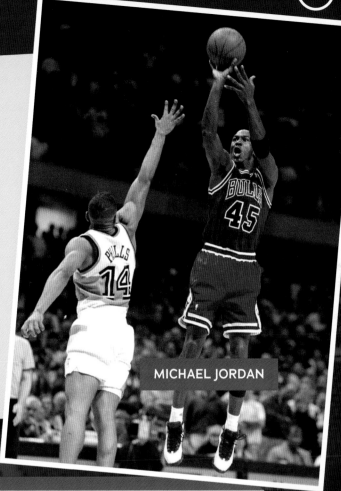

MICHAEL JORDAN

Most NBA Career Points Scored

PLAYER	TEAM*	POINTS
Kareem Abdul-Jabbar	Los Angeles Lakers	38,387
Karl Malone	Utah Jazz	36,928
Kobe Bryant	Los Angeles Lakers	33,643
Michael Jordan	Chicago Bulls	32,292
Wilt Chamberlain	Philadelphia Warriors	31,419
Dirk Nowitzki	Dallas Mavericks	29,491
Shaquille O'Neal	Los Angeles Lakers	28,596
Moses Malone	Houston Rockets	27,409
Elvin Hayes	Washington Bullets	27,313
Hakeem Olajuwon	Houston Rockets	26,946

*The player spent most of his career with this team.

INSTANT SUCCESS

The Women's National Basketball Association (WNBA) began its first season with eight teams in June 1997. The league quickly became a success. By 1999 games averaged 10,000 fans and were shown on TV in 125 countries. And by 2000, the league had doubled in size to include 16 teams. The league's first-ever **draft** pick, Tina Thompson, played for 17 seasons—and became the league's all-time scoring leader.

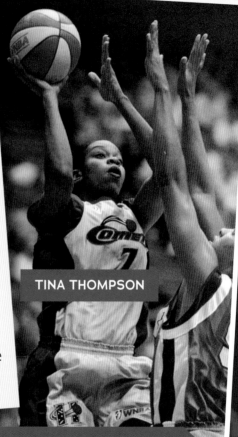

TINA THOMPSON

Most WNBA Career Points Scored

PLAYER	TEAM*	POINTS
Tina Thompson	Houston Comets	7,488
Tamika Catchings	Indiana Fever	7,380
Diana Taurasi	Phoenix Mercury	7,311
Katie Smith	Minnesota Lynx	6,452
Cappie Pondexter	New York Liberty	6,312
Lisa Leslie	Los Angeles Sparks	6,263
Lauren Jackson	Seattle Storm	6,007
Becky Hammon	San Antonio Stars	5,841
DeLisha Milton-Jones	Los Angeles Sparks	5,571
Katie Douglas	Connecticut Sun	5,560

*The player spent most of her career with this team.

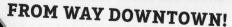

FROM WAY DOWNTOWN!

The **three-point shot** was originally used by a league known as the American Basketball Association (ABA). When the ABA and NBA merged in 1976, NBA coaches and officials did not want to include the shot. They thought it would lead to boring basketball. But fans thought three-pointers were exciting. In 1979 the NBA adopted the three-point shot. On October 12, 1979, Chris Ford of the Boston Celtics made the first three-pointer in NBA history. Since then players have become better at shooting three-pointers, and it has become one of the best ways for a team to score lots of points quickly.

STEPHEN CURRY

Most Three-Pointers in a Season

PLAYER	TEAM	SEASON	THREE-POINTERS
Stephen Curry	Golden State Warriors	2015–2016	402
Stephen Curry	Golden State Warriors	2014–2015	286
Klay Thompson	Golden State Warriors	2015–2016	276
Stephen Curry	Golden State Warriors	2012–2013	272
Ray Allen	Seattle SuperSonics	2005–2006	269

Most Three-Pointers in a Career

PLAYER	TEAM*	THREE-POINTERS
Ray Allen	Milwaukee Bucks	2,973
Reggie Miller	Indiana Pacers	2,560
Jason Terry	Dallas Mavericks	2,169
Paul Pierce	Boston Celtics	2,128
Jason Kidd	Dallas Mavericks	1,988

*The player spent most of his career with this team.

GRABBING THE REBOUND

You cannot score unless you have the ball. One way to get the ball is to **rebound** missed shots. You can grab your opponent's miss, known as a defensive rebound, or snatch your own team's miss, called an offensive rebound. Wilt Chamberlain is the all-time leading rebounder with 23,924 rebounds, and Bill Russell of the Boston Celtics is right behind him with 21,620. At 7 feet 1 inch (2.2 m) and 6 feet 9 inches (2.1 m), respectively, they towered over the other players on the court. This gave Chamberlain and Russell a great rebounding advantage.

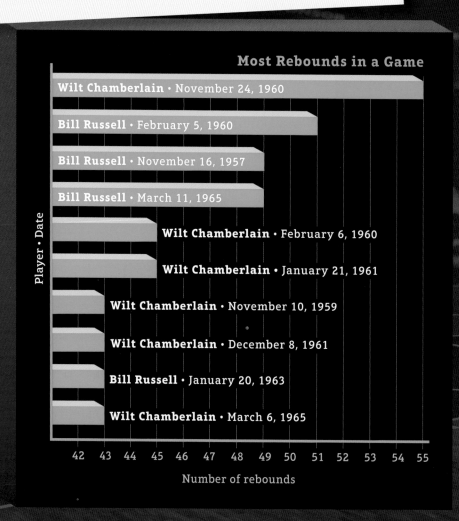

Most Rebounds in a Game

Player • Date	Number of rebounds
Wilt Chamberlain • November 24, 1960	55
Bill Russell • February 5, 1960	51
Bill Russell • November 16, 1957	49
Bill Russell • March 11, 1965	49
Wilt Chamberlain • February 6, 1960	45
Wilt Chamberlain • January 21, 1961	45
Wilt Chamberlain • November 10, 1959	44
Wilt Chamberlain • December 8, 1961	43
Bill Russell • January 20, 1963	43
Wilt Chamberlain • March 6, 1965	43

42 43 44 45 46 47 48 49 50 51 52 53 54 55

WILT CHAMBERLAIN

LARRY STEELE

LIKE A THIEF IN THE NIGHT

Another way to get the ball is to steal it! The best rebounders are generally centers or big power forwards. Steals leaders are usually guards, who are often small and quick. Steals have been part of the game since the beginning, but the NBA did not start recording steals as an official statistic until the 1973–1974 season. The steals leader that first year was Larry Steele, of course.

Most Career Steals

PLAYER	TEAM*	STEALS
John Stockton	Utah Jazz	3,265
Jason Kidd	Dallas Mavericks	2,684
Michael Jordan	Chicago Bulls	2,514
Gary Payton	Seattle SuperSonics	2,445
Maurice Cheeks	Philadelphia 76ers	2,310
Scottie Pippen	Chicago Bulls	2,307
Clyde Drexler	Portland Trail Blazers	2,207
Hakeem Olajuwon	Houston Rockets	2,162
Alvin Robertson	San Antonio Spurs	2,112
Karl Malone	Utah Jazz	2,085

*The player spent most of his career with this team.

GET THAT OUTTA HERE!

The most exciting defensive play in basketball might be the **blocked shot**. Seeing the ball get knocked out of the air excites fans and can give teams a boost. The greatest shot blockers were tall. Hakeem Olajuwon (an even 7 feet tall, or 2.1 m) is the all-time leader in blocked shots. He is shorter than some of the other great shot blockers, but Olajuwon could jump with the best of them.

STATS FACT

Although Muggsy Bogues, at 5 feet 3 inches (1.6 m), was the shortest player ever in the NBA, he still recorded 39 career blocked shots. That includes one block against 7-foot (2.1 m) center Patrick Ewing.

HAKEEM OLAJUWON *(RIGHT)*

Most Blocks in a Career

PLAYER	HEIGHT	TEAM*	BLOCKS
Hakeem Olajuwon	7′ (2.1 m)	Houston Rockets	3,830
Dikembe Mutombo	7′2″ (2.2 m)	Denver Nuggets	3,289
Kareem Abdul-Jabbar	7′2″ (2.2 m)	Los Angeles Lakers	3,189
Mark Eaton	7′4″ (2.2 m)	Utah Jazz	3,064

*The player spent most of his career with this team.

Most Blocks in a Game

PLAYER	HEIGHT	TEAM	BLOCKS	DATE
Elmore Smith	7′ (2.1 m)	Los Angeles Lakers	17	October 28, 1973
Shaquille O'Neal	7′1″ (2.1 m)	Orlando Magic	15	November 20, 19
Manute Bol	7′7″ (2.3 m)	Washington Bullets	15	February 26, 198
Manute Bol	7′7″ (2.3 m)	Washington Bullets	15	January 25, 1986

HE CAN DO IT ALL

Basketball fans usually focus on five main statistics. These are points, rebounds, assists, steals, and blocked shots. Reaching double digits (10 or more) in any of those stats is good. Reaching double digits in three of the categories is called a **triple-double**, and it is rare. In an amazing 1961–1962 season, Oscar Robertson of the Cincinnati Royals averaged a triple-double (30.8 points, 11.4 assists, and 12.5 rebounds) for the *entire season*!

Triple-Double Leaders for the 2015–2016 Season

PLAYER	TEAM	TRIPLE-DOUBLES
Russell Westbrook	Oklahoma City Thunder	18
Draymond Green	Golden State Warriors	13
Rajon Rondo	Sacramento Kings	6
Giannis Antetokounmpo	Milwaukee Bucks	5
John Wall	Washington Wizards	4
James Harden	Houston Rockets	3
LeBron James	Cleveland Cavaliers	3
Hassan Whiteside	Miami Heat	3
Nicolas Batum	Charlotte Hornets	2
Jimmy Butler	Chicago Bulls	2
Stephen Curry	Golden State Warriors	2
Pau Gasol	Chicago Bulls	2

BEST OF THE BEST

The NBA MVP award has been presented every year since 1956 to the best player of the regular season. Until 1980 the award was decided by a player vote. Starting in 1981, the winner has been selected by a group of sportswriters and broadcasters. Of the 31 players to win the trophy, 13 have won it more than once. Players become eligible to be inducted into the Naismith Memorial Basketball Hall of Fame four years after retirement. Every eligible MVP winner is in the Hall of Fame.

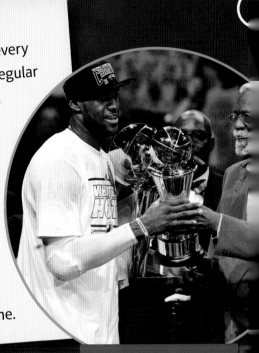

LEBRON JAMES *(LEFT)*

STATS FACT

In 2016 Golden State Warriors star Stephen Curry became the only unanimous selection for MVP—he was every voter's first choice. Only three other players have ever come within five votes of a unanimous selection.

p MVP Winners

P ARDS	PLAYER	TEAM*	MVP SEASONS
	Kareem Abdul-Jabbar	Los Angeles Lakers	1971, 1972, 1974, 1976, 1977, 1980
	Michael Jordan	Chicago Bulls	1988, 1991, 1992, 1996, 1998
	Bill Russell	Boston Celtics	1958, 1961, 1962, 1963, 1965
	LeBron James	Cleveland Cavaliers	2009, 2010, 2012, 2013
	Wilt Chamberlain	Philadelphia Warriors	1960, 1966, 1967, 1968

player spent most of his career with this team.

CHAPTER TWO

TEAM SUPER STATS

WINNING IS EVERYTHING

The San Antonio Spurs joined the NBA for the 1976–1977 season. In the 40 seasons since then, the Spurs have missed the playoffs only four times. They have a winning regular-season record against every other NBA team. Of the NBA's 30 teams, 13 have all-time winning records. If you don't see your favorite team on this page, the team likely has an all-time winning percentage under .500, which means they've lost more games than they've won.

2013–2014 SAN ANTONIO SPURS

Best All-Time Records

TEAM	RECORD	WINNING PERCENTAGE
San Antonio Spurs	2,006–1,226	.621
Los Angeles Lakers	3,235–2,134	.603
Boston Celtics	3,221–2,257	.588
Phoenix Suns	2,122–1,766	.546
Oklahoma City Thunder	2,139–1,831	.539
Portland Trail Blazers	1,991–1,733	.535
Utah Jazz	1,815–1,581	.534
Chicago Bulls	2,115–1,936	.522
Miami Heat	1,170–1,078	.520
Houston Rockets	2,052–1,918	.517

RECORD-BREAKING RECORDS

The Golden State Warriors were in the spotlight in 2015–2016 as they pursued the best regular-season record in NBA history. On the last day of the regular season, they overtook the win total set by the Chicago Bulls 20 years earlier. But after losing only nine games in the regular season, the Warriors lost to the Cleveland Cavaliers in the NBA Finals.

2015–2016 GOLDEN STATE WARRIORS

Best Regular-Season Records

YEAR	TEAM	RECORD	PLAYOFF RESULT
2015–2016	Golden State Warriors	73–9	Lost NBA Finals
1995–1996	Chicago Bulls	72–10	Won NBA title
1996–1997	Chicago Bulls	69–13	Won NBA title
1971–1972	Los Angeles Lakers	69–13	Won NBA title
1966–1967	Philadelphia 76ers	68–13	Won NBA title
1972–1973	Boston Celtics	68–14	Lost Eastern Conference Finals
1985–1986	Boston Celtics	67–15	Won NBA title
1991–1992	Chicago Bulls	67–15	Won NBA title
1999–2000	Los Angeles Lakers	67–15	Won NBA title
2014–2015	Golden State Warriors	67–15	Won NBA title
2006–2007	Dallas Mavericks	67–15	Lost Western Conference first round
2015–2016	San Antonio Spurs	67–15	Lost Western Conference Semifinals

LIFTING THE TROPHY!

The goal for NBA teams is to raise the Larry O'Brien NBA Championship Trophy, the award presented each year to the NBA champions. The Boston Celtics, led by coach Red Auerbach and center Bill Russell, won 11 titles in 13 years. That included eight straight championships from 1958–1959 to 1965–1966. The Minneapolis Lakers won five titles in six years. After the team moved to Los Angeles, the Lakers won five championships in the 1980s and five more in the 2000s.

HOUSTON COMETS

STATS FACT
The Houston Comets won first four WNBA champio becoming only the fifth professional sports team four championships in a

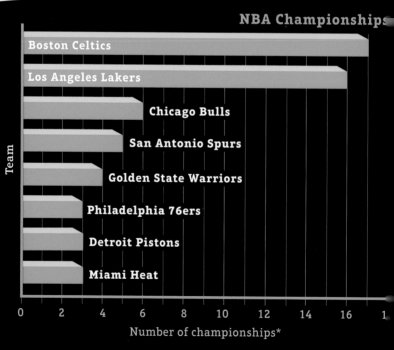

NBA Championships

Team

Boston Celtics
Los Angeles Lakers
Chicago Bulls
San Antonio Spurs
Golden State Warriors
Philadelphia 76ers
Detroit Pistons
Miami Heat

0 2 4 6 8 10 12 14 16 1
Number of championships*

*Includes titles won while representing other cities

CAN'T STAND LOSING

Los Angeles Lakers team captain Elgin Baylor was injured early in the 1971–1972 season and retired after 14 seasons in the NBA. But fans had nothing to worry about. Led by Wilt Chamberlain and Jerry West, the Lakers won 33 games in a row that season. It was the longest winning streak ever in a major pro sport. The Miami Heat, with stars LeBron James and Dwyane Wade, threatened the record in the 2012–2013 season. The Golden State Warriors started their 2015–2016 season 24–0 before losing. And the Houston Rockets reached 22 wins without a loss in 2007–2008 despite losing star center Yao Ming to injury midway through the streak.

STATS FACT
In 1996–1997, the Phoenix Suns started the year 0–13. Late in the season, they won 10 straight games to help make the playoffs.

DWYANE WADE

Most Wins in a Row in a Season

TEAM	FIRST GAME OF STREAK	LAST GAME OF STREAK	GAMES WON
Los Angeles Lakers	November 5, 1971	January 7, 1972	33
Miami Heat	February 3, 2013	March 27, 2013	27
Golden State Warriors	October 27, 2015	December 12, 2015	24
Houston Rockets	January 29, 2008	March 18, 2008	22
Milwaukee Bucks	February 6, 1971	March 8, 1971	20
Atlanta Hawks	December 27, 2014	February 2, 2015	19
San Antonio Spurs	February 26, 2014	April 3, 2014	19
Boston Celtics	November 15, 2008	December 25, 2008	19
Los Angeles Lakers	February 4, 2000	March 13, 2000	19

NOT A CHANCE

The 1991–1992 Cleveland Cavaliers wanted revenge. The Miami Heat had beaten them by two points a week earlier in Miami, and the Cavs weren't about to let them win again. The Cavs led the rematch in Cleveland by 20 points at halftime. And that was just the start. The Cavs continued to sink baskets in the second half and went on to win, 148–80. Miami scored the game's last five points, but this contest was still the biggest blowout in NBA history.

1997–1998 INDIANA PACERS AN
PORTLAND TRAIL BLAZERS

Biggest Margins of Victory in NBA History

DATE	WINNING TEAM	LOSING TEAM	SCORE
December 17, 1991	Cleveland Cavaliers	Miami Heat	148–80
February 27, 1998	Indiana Pacers	Portland Trail Blazers	124–59
March 19, 1972	Los Angeles Lakers	Golden State Warriors	162–99
November 2, 1991	Golden State Warriors	Sacramento Kings	153–91
December 25, 1960	Syracuse Nationals	New York Knicks	162–100
December 26, 1978	Milwaukee Bucks	Detroit Pistons	143–84
March 19, 1977	Golden State Warriors	Indiana Pacers	150–91
April 27, 2009	Denver Nuggets	New Orleans Hornets	121–63
December 29, 1992	Sacramento Kings	Dallas Mavericks	139–81
December 15, 1985	Milwaukee Bucks	Sacramento Kings	140–82

THE WINNINGEST LOSERS

The 1975–1976 Detroit Pistons had a losing record, yet they still made the playoffs. Then they won their first playoff series, 2 games to 1. Their opponent, the Milwaukee Bucks, also had a losing record, so maybe it wasn't such a surprising win. No team with a losing record ever won a playoff series again.

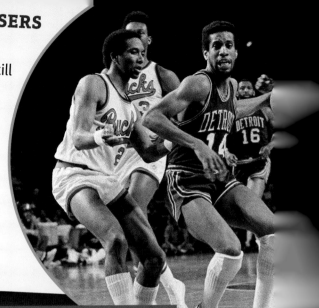

1975–1976 DETROIT PISTONS AND MILWAUKEE BUCKS

Playoff Teams with the Worst Regular-Season Records since 1976–1977

SEASON	TEAM	RECORD	PLAYOFF RESULT
1985–1986	Chicago Bulls	30–52	Lost in first round
1987–1988	San Antonio Spurs	31–51	Lost in first round
1994–1995	Boston Celtics	35–47	Lost in first round
1985–1986	San Antonio Spurs	35–47	Lost in first round
1983–1984	Washington Bullets	35–47	Lost in first round
2003–2004	Boston Celtics	36–46	Lost in first round
1996–1997	Los Angeles Clippers	36–46	Lost in first round
1984–1985	Cleveland Cavaliers	36–46	Lost in first round
1984–1985	Phoenix Suns	36–46	Lost in first round

CHAPTER THREE

STATS ARE HERE TO STAY

THE BOX SCORE

A box score is a chart that contains statistics from a game. By looking at a box score, fans can quickly find out everything they want to know about that game. Use the key to read the box score on the next page.

In the 1940s, an elementary school student named Dick Pfander began collecting box scores from newspapers. Pfander's interest in box scores grew, and he spent 40 years searching for—and finding—the box score of every NBA game ever played. He donated his collection to the website basketball-reference.com.

DRAYMOND GREEN
(RIGHT)

Key

FGM-A = field goals made-attempted	
3PM-A = three-pointers made-attempted	
FTM-A = free throws made-attempted	
REB = rebounds	
AST = assists	
STL = steals	
BLK = blocks	
PTS = points	

Golden State Warriors

PLAYER	FGM-A	3PM-A	FTM-A	REB	AST	STL	BLK	PTS
Harrison Barnes	5–8	1–1	0–0	6	3	0	0	11
Andrew Bogut	2–2	0–0	0–0	6	1	1	0	4
Stephen Curry	9–15	5–8	5–5	2	3	1	0	28
Draymond Green	4–9	2–4	0–0	8	7	1	2	10
Klay Thompson	5–17	2–8	3–4	2	4	1	0	15
Leandro Barbosa	2–6	0–1	0–0	2	2	2	0	4
Ian Clark	0–3	0–1	1–2	0	1	0	0	1
Festus Ezeli	5–5	0–0	2–6	5	1	0	1	12
Andre Iguodala	4–10	1–3	5–6	3	1	3	0	14
Shaun Livingston	1–3	0–0	0–0	4	3	0	0	2
Brandon Rush	0–0	0–0	0–0	1	0	0	0	0
Marreese Speights	5–6	2–2	1–2	2	0	0	0	13
Anderson Varejao	1–1	0–0	2–3	4	0	0	0	4

STAT STRATEGY

Stats aren't only read by fans who love the game. Players, coaches, and **analysts** also read and examine stats to improve their play and knowledge of basketball. Coaches use statistics to plan and form strategies. In 2004 the first statistical analyst was hired by an NBA team full-time. In 2013 the NBA installed six cameras in the rafters of every NBA arena. These cameras track players and help record accurate statistics about dribbling, shooting, and many other aspects of the game.

One way players use these stats is to plan ways to guard opponents. For instance, if a player knows he is defending an opponent who is great at making three-pointers, the player will guard that opponent more closely at the three-point line. But if the opponent has a low three-point shooting percentage, the defender knows he can back off when the opponent is far away from the basket.

FANTASY AND THE FUTURE

Fantasy basketball is a contest that adult fans play using the real statis of NBA players. To play in a fantasy league, fans draft players to form teams. Drafts are conducted online or in person. Fantasy teams win or lo based on how well their players perform. One study showed that nearly in five adults in the United States plays fantasy sports.

As the popularity of stats among fans and those involved in the game continues to grow, it is likely that the game will change too. In recent ears, stats analysis has led to players taking more three-point shots and hanging their defensive tactics. Players may develop other new strategie s well. And the NBA may respond by adjusting its rules to maintain fair ay. For instance, it has become common for players to foul poor free row shooters late in a game, hoping the player will miss the free throws. ague officials are discussing rules changes to keep this tactic from being ed. It will be fun to watch how statistics continue to affect the game.

STATS MATCHUP

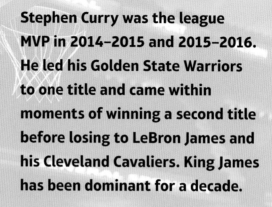

Stephen Curry was the league MVP in 2014–2015 and 2015–2016. He led his Golden State Warriors to one title and came within moments of winning a second title before losing to LeBron James and his Cleveland Cavaliers. King James has been dominant for a decade.

Stephen Curry Golden State Warriors	
2,375	Points
30.1	Scoring average
.504	Field goal percentage
402	Three-pointers made
.908	Free throw percentage
5.4	Rebounds
6.7	Assists
2.1	Steals
0.2	Blocks

STEPHEN CURRY

James has been the league MVP four times and his teams have won three titles. Here are the superstars' stats for the 2015–2016 season. Who is the greater player? You decide.

LeBron James
Cleveland Cavaliers

1,920	Points
25.3	Scoring average
.520	Field goal percentage
87	Three-pointers made
.731	Free throw percentage
7.4	Rebounds
6.8	Assists
1.4	Steals
0.6	Blocks

LEBRON JAMES

analysts: people whose job it is to study statistics and form opinions based on the data

blocked shot: a defensive play in which a shot is tipped or swatted on its way to the basket

draft: a yearly event during which professional teams choose new players

free throws: unopposed shots taken by a player who has been fouled by an opponent

rebound: to gain possession of a missed shot

rookies: players in their first year in the NBA

shot clock: a 24-second timer that begins as soon as a team takes possession of the ball. If a team doesn't hit the backboard or rim with a shot within 24 seconds, the other team takes possession of the ball.

three-point shot: a shot that is taken from behind the three-point line, worth three points

triple-double: achieving 10 or more points in three statistical categories

Basketball Reference
http://www.basketball-reference.com

ESPN Basketball
http://www.espn.com/nba/statistics

Fishman, Jon M. *LeBron James*. Minneapolis: Lerner Publications, 2018.

Land of Basketball
http://www.landofbasketball.com

National Basketball Association
http://www.nba.com

Savage, Jeff. *Super Basketball Infographics*. Minneapolis: Lerner Publications, 2015.

Tejada, Justin. *Sports Illustrated Kids Stats! The Greatest Numbers in Sports*. New York: Time Home Entertainment, 2013.

PHOTO ACKNOWLEDGMENTS

The images in this book are used with the permission of: © iStockphoto.com/Pali Rao, p. 1; © iStockphoto.com/sArhange1 (basketball court background throughout); © Bettmann/Getty Images, pp. 4, 13; © New York Daily News Archive/Getty Images, p. 5; © Andrew D. Bernstein/National Basketball Association/Getty Images, p. 6; © Laura Westlund/Independent Picture Service, pp. 7, 8, 12, 20 (bar graph); AP Photo/ Tony Dejak, p. 9; © Doug Pensinger/Getty Images, p. 10; JOHN G. MABANGLO/EPA/ Newscom, p. 11; © Rogers Photo Archive/Getty Images, p. 14; AP Photo/David J. Phillip, p. 15; AP Photo/Sue Ogrocki, p. 16; Fang Zhe Xinhua News Agency/Newscom, p. 17; ASHLEY LANDIS/EPA/Newscom, p. 18; AP Photo/Marcio Jose Sanchez, p. 19; AP Photo/ Pat Sullivan, p. 20 (top); David Santiago/ABACAUSA.COM/Newscom, p. 21; © JOHN RUTHROFF/AFP/Getty Images, p. 22; AP Photo, p. 23; AP Photo/George Nikitin, p. 24; © Michael Reaves/Getty Images, p. 26; © The Washington Post/Getty Images, p. 27; LARRY W. SMITH/EPA/Newscom, p. 28; DAVID MAXWELL/EPA/Newscom, p. 29.

Front cover: © iStockphoto.com/Pali Rao.

Back cover: © iStockphoto.com/sArhange1 (basketball court background).